Getting To Know
Your Rabbit

Getting To Know Your Rabbit

Gill Page

INTERPET PUBLISHING

The Author

Gill Page has been involved with a wide variety of animals for many years. She has run a successful pet centre and for some time helped in rescuing and re-homing unwanted animals. She has cared for many animals of her own and is keen to pass on her experience so that children may learn how to look after their pets lovingly and responsibly.

Published by Interpet Publishing,
Vincent Lane,
Dorking,
Surrey RH4 3YX,
England

© 2000 Interpet Publishing Ltd.

ISBN 1-84286-110-7

The recommendations in this book are given without any guarantees on the part of the author and publisher. If in doubt, seek the advice of a vet or pet-care specialist.

Credits

Editor: Philip de Ste. Croix

Designer: Phil Clucas MSIAD

Studio photography: Neil Sutherland

Colour artwork: Rod Ferring

Production management: Consortium, Poslingford, Suffolk CO10 8RA

Print production: SNP Leefung, China

Printed and bound in the Far East

Contents

Making Friends   6
Getting To Know Me   8
Choosing Me   10
Taking Me Home   12
Holding Me Safely   14
My Own House   16
Time For Bed   18
My Favourite Foods   20
Nice and Fresh   22
Meal Times   24
Treats and Titbits   26
My Animal Friends   28
Toys and Playtime   30
Looking My Best   32
Safety In The Garden   34
Safety In The House   36
Visits To My Doctor   38
If I Have Babies   40
My Special Page   42
Rabbit Check List   43
My Relations   44
A Note To Parents   46
Acknowledgements   48

Making Friends

Hello. I am your new friend. What is your name? If you give me a short name, I will soon learn when you are calling me. When I come to live with you, I will be very small and I can be easily hurt. Please do not treat me like a toy. If I am tired, pop me into my house, where I will go to sleep for a while. I will soon wake up again and be ready to play more games with you.

It is such fun playing games, like hide and seek.

I try very hard to keep my fur
clean and tidy. You can help
me by brushing my coat with
my very own brush. I like being
stroked, but I can get a bit
worried about being picked up.
Please will you feed me every day
and make sure I have lots of clean
water to drink. I would like a nice,
big house of my own to live in.
I will be lonely living alone, so I would
really like to have a guinea pig or
another rabbit as a friend to live
with me. A safe place to play in
the garden will give me
plenty of room to run
around. I know that
soon we will be
good friends.

We are
going to be
really good
friends.

Rabbits with long, floppy ears are called "lop-eared rabbits".

Getting To Know Me

I have short hair that can be all sorts of different colours.
I may be black, grey, chocolate, white or many other
shades. I can have white fur with spots, stripes and patches
of a different colour. My ears can be short or long. They
will either stick straight up or droop down. If I have droopy
ears, I will be called a lop-eared rabbit. I may be a small
friend or I might grow to be enormous! A girl rabbit is
called a "doe" and a boy rabbit is called a "buck".

My tail is called a "scut".

My front feet are small, but my back feet are much bigger. My strong back feet help me to hop along the ground and to jump over things. I have a small fluffy tail – it is called a "scut". I have long, sharp teeth at the front of my mouth. These teeth keep growing all the time so I need lots of hard things to chew to keep them short. I have long whiskers and my nose twitches a lot. I will soon learn to love being stroked and cuddled by you, but being picked up can be a bit scary at first.

We are the same breed, but have different colour fur.

Choosing Me

You can buy me from a pet shop or from a person who breeds rabbits at their home. Animal rescue centres often have rabbits like me that need a new home. Long-haired rabbits look very cute and cuddly, but they can be very hard to take care of. Short-haired friends like me are much easier to look after. I should have bright, shiny eyes and my teeth should look clean and straight.

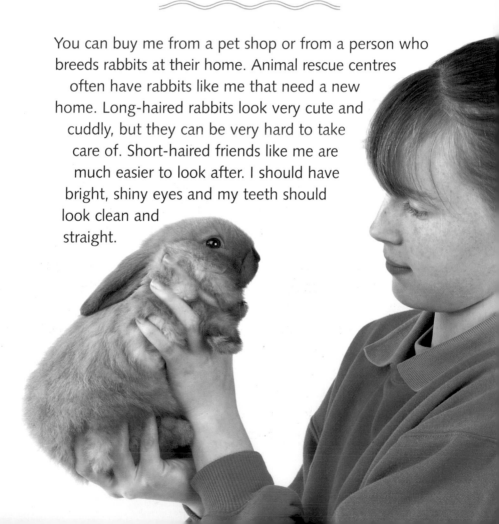

I would like a friend to keep me company; another rabbit or a guinea pig would make me happy.

Is my fur clean? There should be no bald patches or insects in my fur. Look in my ears. They should be as clean as your own.

Ask if you can hold me. If I feel thin and bony, I may be ill. I should be hopping around in my pen, not sitting very quietly in a corner. I really do not like living on my own, so please choose two of us. Two sisters or two brothers will usually live together happily. Never buy a girl and a boy to live together as they will always be having babies. Instead of just two rabbits, you will have hundreds! If you do not want to keep two rabbits, you can buy a guinea pig that is the same age as me.

Taking Me Home

I will need a box in which I will be safe for the journey
home. A basket made of plastic or wire is best. I can
chew my way out of a cardboard one very quickly. Put
bedding in the bottom of the box, as that will stop me
from slipping and sliding about. Please have my new
house ready for me when you come to pick me up. I will
need food, hay, water and bedding. As soon as we are
home, pop me into my house and leave me to rest.
I might hide in my bedding for a while. I will explore my
cage, eat my food and have a drink of water when
I think that nobody is watching me.

For a few days leave me in my cage. If you talk quietly to me when we are together, I will soon know that you are my friend. Offer me a piece of carrot or apple; I may be very brave and take it from your hand. When I have settled down, you can put me outdoors in my play area or let me run around in your room. I need lots of exercise and get so bored if I am shut in my house all day long.

I will soon get to know you and we can be friends.

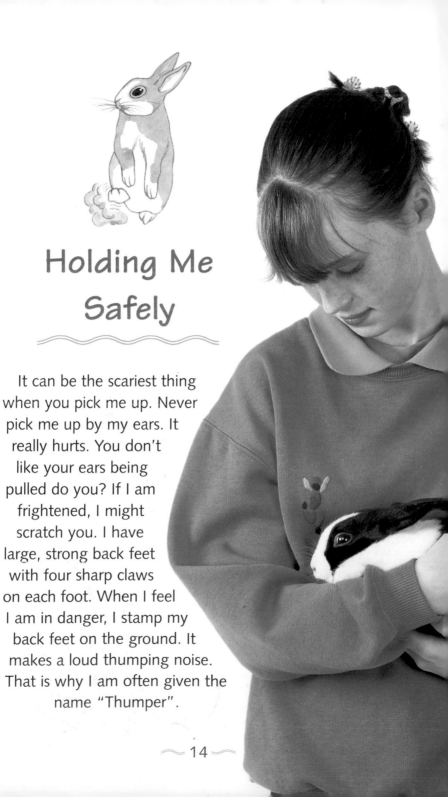

Holding Me Safely

It can be the scariest thing when you pick me up. Never pick me up by my ears. It really hurts. You don't like your ears being pulled do you? If I am frightened, I might scratch you. I have large, strong back feet with four sharp claws on each foot. When I feel I am in danger, I stamp my back feet on the ground. It makes a loud thumping noise. That is why I am often given the name "Thumper".

I must learn that I will be quite safe when you
pick me up. Sit on the floor and hold me in your
lap. When I am happy to sit and be stroked, you can
try gently picking me up. Put one hand under my
bottom and the other gently around my neck and hold
me close to you. I may never learn to enjoy being picked
up. In that case you can teach me to hop into a bucket
(put straw in the bottom first) and then you can carry me
around in it. If you are a little person, choose a friend
that will not grow too heavy for you to carry. A Dutch
rabbit or a Dwarf
Lop will not get
too big.

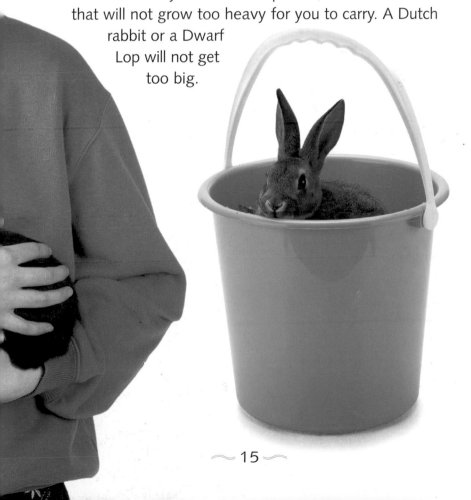

My Own House

My house can be made of plastic and wire. I use it as my bedroom if I actually live inside your home. Another sort of house is made of wood and it is called a hutch. It has a sloping roof with special material on it that keeps the rain out. It has two doors. The wooden one is my bedroom door. The other is made of wire netting, so that I can see outside. I often sit up on my back legs, so when you buy a hutch or cage, measure it to see that it is tall enough. If it isn't, I will keep banging my head on the roof. Ouch! That has given me a headache.

I like to snuggle down in the straw of my hutch.

Stand the hutch off the ground or it will be too draughty and damp for me. I need a safe place to play and eat in the garden. A run, or something called an ark, keeps me safe from danger. One end of my pen should be covered in wood so that I can shelter in there, away from the hot sun and the rain. In warm weather I can live outside in my hutch. When it is cold, please put my house into a warm shed or I can live with you indoors.

Time for Bed

I do like a soft and cosy bed to snuggle in but I don't use sheets and a duvet for my bedding, like you do. I would rather have clean, dry straw. Put some wood shavings or newspaper on the bottom of my house – this will soak up any wet patches. Then put a big pile of straw on the top. I can snuggle down in the straw at bedtime. You can use wood shavings only, but they do seem to get stuck in my fur. They even find their way into my food bowl and I hate eating shavings.

Dry straw

Wood shavings

You will have to clean my house for me every day. If you don't, it will become very smelly and I hate that. Put me in my outdoor run or my carry case while you clean out my house. Clear out the dirty bits and throw them away. Then add fresh bedding. When you put me back into my house, I will push the straw around to make it really comfortable. Every month you can throw all the bedding away and give my house a really good scrub. Always make sure my house is dry before you put new bedding, and me, back into it.

You will need to clean out and scrub my hutch every month.

Rabbit pellets

Chopped hay

Alfalfa hay

Rabbit mix

My Favourite Foods

Before you bring me home, find out which dry food
I have been eating. Buy some of the same food to take
home with me so that I will have food I like in my new
home. Ask if I have been eating fresh food and grass.
If I haven't, only feed me a little grass or other fresh food
to begin with (see pages 22-23). As my tummy gets used
to the fresh food, you can feed me with more of it.

There are two types of dry food that I like. One is called
a rabbit mix. It is very colourful with bits of food of all
sorts of shapes and sizes in it. I can pick out and eat my
favourite bits first. Rabbit pellets are very good for me.

They do look a bit boring – but they are very tasty.
I need to eat my dry food every day. It helps to keep me
feeling good. I like to eat hay as well. Hay is dried grass.
Put the hay in a little rack fixed to the side of my hutch.
I can nibble it whenever I want to. If the hay is on the
floor, I will sit on it and spoil it.

Tomato

Apple

Carrot

Broccoli

Nice and Fresh

I can eat a lot of fresh fruits, nuts and vegetables. Carrots, parsnips and swedes are hard, crunchy vegetables that are really great for my teeth. Green vegetables are the ones I like the best, but too many can give me a tummy ache. Green cabbage, peas and spinach are also good for me. I like apples, pears, tomatoes and a little piece of melon. As an extra special treat I could have just one small strawberry. I can spend ages crunching up sunflower seeds. Grass is very important for me. If my outdoor run is put on a fresh part of the lawn every day, I can eat as much as I want. I will even eat plants that you think are weeds.

I love parsnips, cabbage leaves, carrots, baby sweetcorn and peas, but only fresh vegetables please.

Always wash my fresh food in clean water.

Dandelion flowers are so yummy. I like the leaves as well. Other weeds I enjoy are chickweed, cow parsley, clover and plantain. In the winter, when it might be too wet or cold to go on the lawn, I will need to eat a few more green vegetables. Please only use fresh food. I like it washed before I eat it. Always ask a grown-up before you pick any wild food for me to eat to make sure that it will not harm me.

Clover

Dandelion leaves

Chickweed

Cow parsley

Dandelion flowers

Plantain

Meal Times

I can be rather clumsy when I am eating my food. Sometimes I stand in my bowl and the food goes all over the floor. Buy a china bowl and it will be too heavy for me to tip over. I need one bowl for my dry food and another for fresh stuff. My bowls should be washed every day. If the bowl is dirty, it has a horrible smell – that makes my whiskers curl! A wire rack hangs on my cage for my hay. I drink quite a lot of water. A water bottle fixed to the cage keeps my water clean and I can have a drink when I am thirsty. Change the water every day – I do like it to taste fresh.

Feeding Timetable

Feed me twice a day – I like to eat at the same time every day. I will know if you are late with my food. My dry food can be left in my bowl all day and night. I can nibble it whenever I feel hungry. Put my fresh food in the bowl at breakfast time. Take out any bits that I have left in the evening. I need about 85 grams (3oz) of fresh food every day.

Breakfast

Throw away any food left over from the day before. Fill my bowl with rabbit mix or pellets. Put chopped-up fresh food in the other bowl. Put hay in the rack. Fill up my water bottle with fresh water.

Dinner

Top up my bowl with extra dry food. Take away any fruit and vegetables left over from breakfast. Make sure that my hay rack is full. Check the water bottle. Is it full of water?

Treats and Titbits

Do you like sweets? They are a lovely treat for you.
I have my own treats that you can buy for me. I must
not eat too many though, or I may get toothache. Some
have nuts or honey on them, others have fruit. Alfalfa
hay is a special treat, but I must only have a little each
week or I will get a tummy ache.

*I love to nibble
the bark of an
apple twig.*

Seed cake treat

Mineral block

Cereal squares

Sunflower seeds

Yoghurt drops

I need to gnaw something hard every day to keep my teeth in good shape. Do you have a fruit tree growing in your garden? Please may I have a small branch? I love nibbling the bark. Hazel and apple wood are my favourites. Not all trees are good for me though, so ask a grown-up to check before you give anything new to me. If I don't have things to chew, my teeth will grow so long I will not be able to eat at all. Mineral blocks can be hung up in my cage. When I chew them, it sharpens my teeth and gives me healthy minerals at the same time. Add vitamin drops to my food once or twice a week to keep me healthy. Read the instructions first, or ask a grown-up to read them for you.

Mineral wheel

Popcorn stick

My Animal Friends

I do not like living on my own. I know we shall be good friends and you will play with me, but I would still like an animal friend to live with. It is easier to buy two of us at the same time from the same place. I will not be lonely when you are not there to play with me. Sisters can live together happily. Brothers will also live together, but you should take them to the veterinary clinic first to have a special operation or they may fight. Never have boys and girls living together. There will soon be hundreds of us running around. There will not be enough room in the house for us all and looking after us will use up all your pocket money.

I like to have a friend to play with.

I also like having a guinea pig as a friend. Then I will have somebody to cuddle up to at bedtime. It can be either a girl or a boy and should be about the same age as me, or a little older. You can help me make friends with any other pets that are living with you, but never, ever, leave me alone with them. Dogs or cats could kill me if you do not watch them carefully.

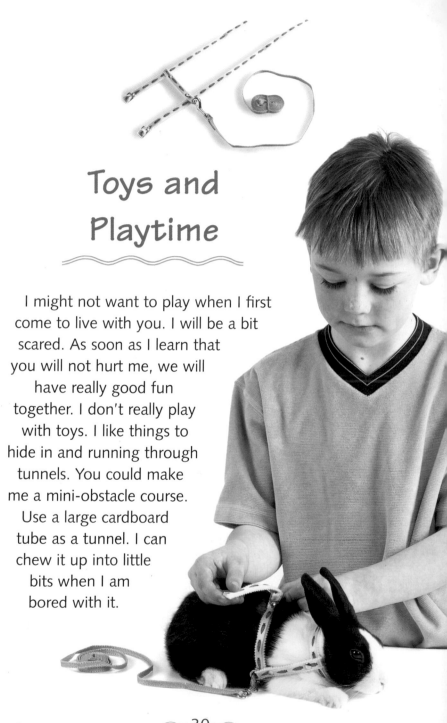

Toys and Playtime

I might not want to play when I first come to live with you. I will be a bit scared. As soon as I learn that you will not hurt me, we will have really good fun together. I don't really play with toys. I like things to hide in and running through tunnels. You could make me a mini-obstacle course. Use a large cardboard tube as a tunnel. I can chew it up into little bits when I am bored with it.

Flower pots are good for playing hide and seek. I can jump over an old broom head. I like to explore piles of stones. A log makes a good lookout post – I can climb on it, sit up on my back legs and have a good look around.
I love digging. Put some soil in a large bucket and I can dig holes in it.
I must always play in a safe place. Shut me in my hutch or run when our games are over. If you teach me to wear a harness, we could go for walks around the garden. All this play has made me very sleepy. I think I will just go and lie down.

This fun ball is my favourite toy. Guess which hole I will pop out of next.

Looking My Best

I try to keep my fur clean and tidy. I use my front paws to clean my face. You can help me by brushing my coat. A comb and a brush is all I need. As I have short hair, I will only need to be brushed once or twice a week. In the spring and autumn I will moult – I will lose some of my old fur and grow some new. This makes me feel itchy and extra brushing really helps.

You can hold me on your lap to groom me, but it might be easier to brush me when I am sitting on a table. Put me on a towel to stop me slipping.

Are my feet clean ?
Check that my claws
haven't grown too long.

Please brush gently or you might hurt me.

Always brush me gently; it hurts if you are too rough. Begin at my head, just behind my ears, and brush down to my tail. Brush under my tummy too. If I wriggle, it is because I am ticklish. When I am moulting, you could use a comb to help me lose my old fur. Check my feet too. Sometimes mud can get stuck in the fur between my toes. Look under my tail. Bits of straw and dirt become squashed into my fur around my tail.

Safety In The Garden

I need lots of exercise. I get so bored shut in my cage or hutch all the time. When the weather is good I can play in my run outside. The run must have wire all round it so that I cannot escape. If I am safely fenced in, animals that might hurt me will not be able to reach me. Put the run under a tree or in a place where I will be shaded from the hot sun. I can be burnt by the sun – just like you. One end of the run should be made of wood. Put lots of straw in there. If it rains, I can burrow into the straw and keep warm and snug.

In nice weather I love to go out in the fresh air.

Please don't leave me out in the run in a thunderstorm. I hate the noise of fireworks too. The bangs and flashes really scare me. Ask a grown-up to check for any nasty plants growing in the garden. Some plants can make me very ill if I eat them. Look for any sharp things hidden in the grass. Old nails or broken glass could hurt me badly. At night shut me into my hutch. Then move my run to a fresh patch of grass ready for the next day.

Be careful, I can climb over fences!

Safety In The House

In the winter it may be too cold or wet for me to be outside in my run. I will need a play area indoors. If you are going to stay with me, you could let me run around in your room. You will make sure the room is safe for me, won't you? Shut all the doors. I like chewing and scratching things so put away anything I might spoil. See that I cannot reach any electric wires. I will chew those too. Keep me away from fires. I may burn myself.

If you train me, I will use a plastic tray filled with wood shavings as my toilet.

You will be able to house-train me like a cat. Use a plastic tray. Put some shavings in it and some of my dirty bedding. If you show me the litter tray and let me sniff it, I should learn to use it as my toilet. Clean it out every day, but put back just a bit of dirty bedding. Then I will remember what the tray is for. Pick up any house plants and put them high up on a table so that I cannot chew them. Your cat or dog friends must not be left alone with me when I am running around the room. They might hurt me.

Visits To My Doctor

My doctor is called a veterinarian. Vet for short. He will look after me if I am sick. I will have to have an injection every year to stop me getting a horrid disease. I can catch it from wild rabbits. It is called myxomatosis. That is a hard word to say. If you say "mixie", the vet will know what you mean. The vet will cut my claws if they are too long. I must go to the vet to have my teeth checked too. If my front teeth are very long, I will not be able to eat my food properly.

I feel much better when my claws have been cut.

Feel carefully all over my body and face for any lumps, bumps or scratches.

My ears are long and they can become smelly inside. The vet will check my ears and clean them for me. Am I very itchy? Ask the vet to look for fleas or lice. A powder will soon get rid of them. Like all animals, I can have tiny worms living in my tummy. The vet will give me medicine to kill them. I must go to see the vet if I have a runny nose or eyes. When I am feeling sick, I do not eat my food. If that happens, take me to the vet quickly. I will die if I stop eating.

If I Have Babies

I do not want to have babies. Looking after them is very hard work for me. I might have some by accident though, so I will tell you how to care for us all. I will need a quiet place to look after them. I do not like anyone looking at them until they are about a week old. Just feed and water me. Don't try to clean out the cage for a few days.

We were in our mummy's tummy for 31 days.

My babies are born without any fur. For two weeks their eyes are closed, so they cannot see. They cannot hear very well either. I feed them with my milk for five weeks. Extra food for me then, so that I can make lots of milk. When I want to eat or drink, I will leave my babies tucked up in a nest made of my own fur.

When they are three weeks old, you can gently pick them up. At five weeks old they will be hopping about. You can take them away from me then. Put them in a cage together. Watch them eat their dry food. When they are six weeks old, they can eat small bits of fruit and vegetables. At eight weeks of age they are ready to go to their new homes.

My Special Page

My name is
Elaine

My birthday is
September 29th

Am I a boy or a girl?

I am a girl

My colour is

yellow

The colour of my eyes is
dark brown

What breed am I? _?_

My favourite food is
spagety

My favourite game is
snow ball fight

My vet's telephone number is _?_

Please put a
photograph or a
picture of me
here

Another name for me is coney.

Rabbit Check List

Daily
1 Feed and water me.
2 Wash my bowls.
3 Check that my eyes and ears are clean.
4 Clean my house.
5 Play with me.

Weekly
6 Brush me.
7 Scrub out my water bottle.
8 Check my teeth.
9 See that my claws are short, with no splits.
10 Weigh me.

I am a medium-sized rabbit – not too heavy for you to pick up.

My Relations

There are so many breeds of rabbit friends to choose from. The smallest is called a Netherland Dwarf. He has tiny little ears. The largest is called a Flemish Giant, but he is enormous. He will be too big and heavy for you. Small and medium-sized rabbits are easier to care for. Dutch rabbits have a white band of fur around their middle. Their face and bottom will have fur of another colour. Dwarf Lop rabbits can be all one colour or a mixture. If their ears are very long, you must watch to see they do not tread on them.

We have been living with people for about 400 years.

English rabbits are often white with spots and splashes of black or brown. They can have a patch of coloured fur on their noses that is in the shape of a butterfly. Himalayan rabbits have creamy white fur on their bodies. The fur on their ears, noses and feet is black, chocolate or blue. A Rex rabbit has short, very thick fur. A friend with white fur and red eyes is called an Albino. You need not buy a pure bred rabbit. There are lots of crossbred ones. They will be medium-sized and have fur that grows in many different colours.

A Devon Rex rabbit.

A Note To Parents

Having pets is fun and the relationship between child and pet is a magical one. I hope this book will encourage the new, young pet owner to look after their pet responsibly and enjoyably. Obviously parents will have to play a supervisory role, not only in daily care, but also to explain that the new pet is a living being and not a toy. A well-cared-for pet is a happy one and will reward the whole family with unconditional love. Parents also have to bear the financial costs. Veterinary care can be eased with the help of Pet Health Insurance. Most veterinary clinics will have leaflets available about it.

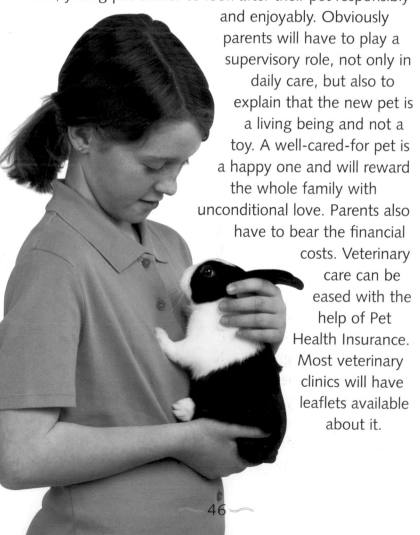

Some of the subjects covered in this book may seem
over-simplified to an adult, but I have tried to avoid too
much technical detail. Rabbits must be checked in the
summer for fly strike. This happens when flies lay their
eggs in the damp fur under their tails. Maggots will
develop and will eat into the flesh of the rabbit,
ultimately killing it. This is definitely a job for an adult.
The subject of giving birth has been touched upon,
but I feel that there are far too many pets being bred
thoughtlessly. Animal rescue centres are often
inundated with unwanted rabbits. Contact your local
centre for information about how to avoid an
unwanted litter of young.

Acknowledgements

The author and publisher would like to thank the owners who generously allowed their pets to be photographed for this book, and the children who agreed to be models. Specifically they would like to thank Florence Elphick – and Clover; Kate Elsom; Caroline Gosden, Sophie King and Claire Watson of Brinsbury College, Adversane – and Daisy and Buttercup; Michael Newman – and Panda and Terminator; Julie White of Holmbush Farm, Faygate. Thanks also to Pet Stop, Billingshurst; Neil Martin and Annika Sumner of Gardens Etc., Washington; Rolf C. Hagen (U.K.) Ltd.; Christy Emblem at Interpet Ltd.; and Farthings Veterinary Group, Billingshurst.

Thanks are due to Damion Diplock at the RSPCA Photolibrary and its photographers who kindly supplied the following photographs that are reproduced in this book.
RSPCA Photolibrary: 9 (E.A. Janes), 40 (Angela Hampton), 41 (Angela Hampton), 44 (Angela Hampton), 45 (Angela Hampton)